GOLDFISH

Maddie Gibbs

PowerKiDS
press™

New York

Published in 2014 by The Rosen Publishing Group, Inc.
29 East 21st Street, New York, NY 10010

First Edition

Editor: Amelie von Zumbusch
Book Design: Andrew Povolny

Photo Credits: Cover, pp. 5, 9 iStockphoto/Thinkstock; p. 7 Gilbert S. Grant/Photo Researchers/Getty Images; p. 11 Jimmy L. L. Tsang/Flickr/Getty Images; p. 13 ori-artiste/Shutterstock.com; p. 15 Julie Mcinnes/Flickr/Getty Images; p. 17 Sami Sarkis/Photographer's Choice RF/Getty Images; p. 19 Doug Martin/Photo Researchers/Getty Images; p. 21 Hemera/Thinkstock; p. 23 Comstock/Comstock Images/Getty Images.

Library of Congress Cataloging-in-Publication Data

Gibbs, Maddie.
 Goldfish / by Maddie Gibbs. — 1st ed.
    p. cm. — (PowerKids Readers. Fun fish)
 Includes bibliographical references and index.
 ISBN 978-1-4777-0758-6 (library binding) — ISBN 978-1-4777-0849-1 (pbk.) —
ISBN 978-1-4777-0850-7 (6-pack)
 1. Goldfish—Juvenile literature. I. Title.
 SF458.G6G53 2014
 639.3'7484—dc23

                                2012051002

Manufactured in the United States of America

CPSIA Compliance Information: Batch #S13PK4: For Further Information contact Rosen Publishing, New York, New York at 1-800-237-9932

Contents

Goldfish are pretty.

5

They have **fins**.

They can live for 20 years.

They are in the carp family.

11

They came from China.

13

The first ones were silver.

They eat a lot.

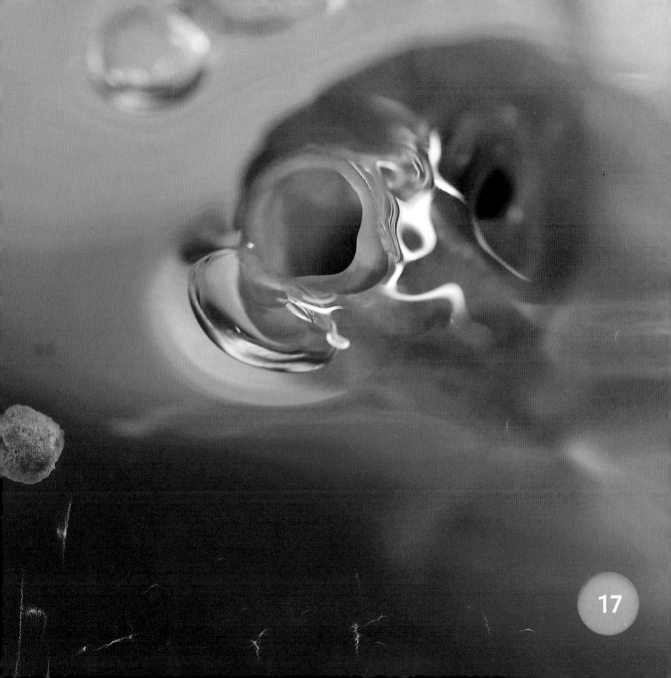

17

Feed them once a day.

Change the water each week.

They are good pets.

WORDS TO KNOW

feed

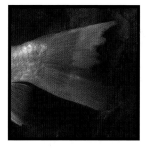
fin

goldfish

INDEX

WEBSITES

Due to the changing nature of Internet links, PowerKids Press has developed an online list of websites related to the subject of this book. This site is updated regularly. Please use this link to access the list:

www.powerkidslinks.com/pkrff/gold/